Speculative Histories

a memoir in essays

Brigitte Lewis

Praise for *Speculative Histories*

When memory fails, what can take its place? Speculation, Brigitte Lewis suggests, other ways of knowing: myth, history, science. Imagination. The quicksilver of language itself. The result is a memoir about what it means to re-member a life. Hybrid in form and lyrical in style, *Speculative Histories* is driven by an authentic voice and singular intelligence. This is a mind on the page, a story unfolding. To read it is to fall in love with what writing can do.
—Beth Alvarado, author of *Jillian in the Borderlands* and *Anxious Attachments*

Reading *Speculative Histories,* I am already thinking how, Persephone-like, I might navigate on the regular between the syntactical landscape and lyric depths of these essays—how I might be made golden, again and again, by Brigitte Lewis' prose. In these essays, revelation does not so much lift the veil as re-spin it from rock and soot and blue, blue water. In these essays, a hole is both absence and substantive, the thing that made it, an opening created by fire (of wood, of neurons, of explosives) or by pick, by carve; or they are a derelict chimney swarming with roses, a snow cave, the blue interior of a balloon, an accommodation of/for breath. I am "highly contaminated by the swoon" of this incandescent work.
— Irene Cooper, author of *Found* and *Committal*

Acknowledgments

Select essays within *Speculative Histories* previously appeared in the following literary magazines thanks to the editors and readers who believed in my work.

"15.5 Paragraphs About Death." *Foglifter*, Issue 3.1. April

2018. "A Bird Knocking Again and Again on a Window." *The Southampton Review*. September 2018.

"Bury." *Flock*, Issue 22. November 2018.

"Melancholy Woman." *The Fanzine*. July 2018.

"Notes > After a Forest Fire." *DIAGRAM*. August 2018.

"Verse." *The Spectacle*. June 2018.

"Wilhelmina." *Permafrost*, Issue 40.1. Winter 2018.

I would also like to thank Beth Alvarado for her belief in my work, vision, and editorial support.

JackLeg Press
www.jacklegpress.org

ISBN: 978-1956907063

Library of Congress Control Number: 2023933890

Cover art: Kristine Snodgrass, glitch series from *Rank (JackLeg, 2021)*

Contents

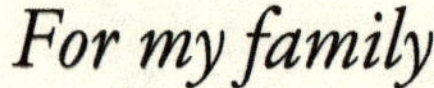

For my family

1

Wilhelmina

I am interested in the bust of Wilhelmina that the Women's Club placed in the local library. I've seen a drawing of her. Round face, broad nose, eyes used to seeing things as they are. Is this what the bust looks like? I search the web to see if the statue still exists, but I only come across a grave marker. Looks like she went by "Minnie."

Sometimes it strikes me as odd how much people bifurcate the weather. Sun is good. Rain is bad. Even if it's a lie, we should probably take the wind at face value. If I'm being honest, though, the windstorms in this town set me on edge. Sometimes, when I go outside after a night of gusts and pulls, other people's trash is pinned to the garage door, and I'm filled with the kind of fear that fashions cyclones.

I know how much I leave out. It both is and is not purposeful. Sometimes, I leave things out because I assume—often wrongly—that something is a given. Sometimes, I leave things out because I can't look at them because they are the sound the wound makes when the wind goes through it, and I make my ears into cotton and hum the tune to XXXXX. Sometimes, I leave things out because I am so tired, and my tongue, hands, and body are broken when it comes to not leaving things out.

In case you don't know, Wilhelmina is dead. She has been dead for over a hundred years, which is nothing, really. Theoretical physicist Carlo Rovelli talks about the difference between *things* and *happenings*. To paraphrase: a *thing* is something that remains equal to itself, like a rock. A *happening* is limited in space and time, like a kiss. But a rock is also a happening from a different vista, sand, and dirt in rock-shaped accretions. In this sense, Wilhelmina is also a *thing* and a *happening*.

As I write this, the wind knocks around my house. Is this a joke? Or would you like to come inside?

She came to North Dakota from Russia, but she wasn't Russian. She was Russian in the same way that I am an American, but really she was German. For five generations, Germans ploughed and tilled around the Volga River and near the Black Sea after invitations from Catherine II and Alexander I to farm southern Russia. I like to think Wilhelmina's people settled near the Black Sea.

And then suddenly, years later, Wilhelmina and her husband John are homesteaders in Ashley, North Dakota. And then, it came on to summer of 1887 (or 1889). And then a prairie fire came along and killed her.

John can make the trip to Ellendale for supplies in two nights and one day. From his horse, he waves toward the sod house where Minnie stays home with their eight children.

Beyond: the prairie stretches incomprehensible. One of the children curls against Wilhelmina while she sleeps. When she sleeps, she sleeps hard but, truthfully, is almost always half awake.

On occasion, Wilhelmina and I have the same dream. It goes one of two ways. In the first one, we are wearing a red hat that has some specific utilitarian purpose. We keep it on when we have to change our clothes. We tell ourselves the hat looks good with the new outfit, but we aren't convinced. In the second dream, we burn alive.

I want to tell you about the beauty of the prairie. About how so much happens between so few distinctions in landscape. The prairie is a series of horizons. The sun is always setting on one of them.

I want to tell you about the beauty of the prairie in Wilhelmina's words: flax and sod and birth and birth and sun-soaked and blizzard-spun and cattle, cattle, love, new, day, again, reap, sow, reap.

Currently, 90% of flax produced in the United States is grown in North Dakota. There, farmers have grown flax since Wilhelmina and John, and the other homesteaders broke the sod, the grass, the roots, the turf. Ten acres of grayish-green leaves and blue-blue flowers can make one of the horizons look like the ocean.

It was either spring or summer in 1887 or 1889. Or both. A typo can point to truth in ways we can't easily discern. And just like that, truth is out to the fields with the cattle, and a prairie fire is in the distance. Smoke in the west since noon, and two of the children had gone to drive truth back home.

Later, the wind shifted, then stilled. The fire moved toward the two children who had gone after the cattle. Smoke stampeded, and both girls held onto a cow's tail. Mary was pulled across the firebreak by her cow. Anna's foot got caught in a gopher hole, and she fell. This was Anna's first time dreaming the dream of being burned alive, and when Wilhelmina got to her, she tore the burning clothes off of her daughter's body.

I understand that fire renews. I understand fire is integral to a thriving prairie ecosystem. Here, plants survive by keeping most of their biomass underground—roots are double or triple (or more) the height of the foliage above. On the surface of the soil, the name Wilhelmina means "resolute protection." No matter how much Minnie and I dig our hands into the earth, we were born to live above ground.

Anna is badly burned. Red skin howling like the day she was born. I take off my apron and tie it around her body. My sweet. My Anna. My honigbiene.

The smoke, the flames block the horizons, swallow the horizons with a hunger so gigantic as to seem cruel. This is the horizon now. Mother and daughter stumble in this horizon and eventually arrive at the sod house that is their sod house among hundreds of sod houses over thousands of acres among tens of thousands of horizons. Anna dies two days later.

Wilhelmina dies two weeks later.

On occasion, Wilhelmina, Anna, and I have the same dream. We wear wings, but we don't always fly. We walk through a scorched landscape, charred and blackened, trees burnt to wrought-iron posts. We walk and walk and walk, never thinking to use our wings. Do you know what it would be? To see this burn from above?

Anna doesn't want to be a statue like her mother. She wants to be painted, preferably in a field of flax. She thinks in oil paints but isn't married to the medium. She asks me if I know any good painters. She asks me how I'd like to be remembered.

I tell her I'm not sure. I tell her maybe some type of auditory art installation. I tell her maybe by something like that field of lightning rods down in White Sands. Or maybe a careful stack of river rock that measures over ten feet tall. Wilhelmina chimes in to say that she didn't have a say in being made into a bust, and why should we get to decide how we're memorialized? Anna is flipping through a Pantone color book, looking for just the right blue for the flax flowers.

Minnie wishes her ashes could have been scattered in the Black Sea. Or, at least, this is what I imagine she wished for, the *thing* of her is buried under the sod, the *happening* of her is a sea bird, diving down, down, wings steady, to fasten her beak around the horizon, to drag it back to her perch, to not swallow it whole, but to rip it apart in tiny bites of light, enjoying the taste of char acquiescing to its fate.

2

Prospecting for Beginners

Do you remember the story of James Marshall at Sutter's Fort? Eureka! And all that? A man who hasn't had enough sleep crouches over a channel of water near his sawmill, the bright of the day green and new upon his neck, when something catches his eye. On the morning of January 24, 1848, Marshall discovered gold in California.

Discovery often lacks volition. For example, the actual location where James Marshall discovered gold is mundane. He hadn't been looking for gold. Still, it is a beautiful spot where the sun glances a path through branches and leafed-out plants to the water. When the sun bounces off of gold, it can throw a spark. What discovery lacks in volition, it sometimes makes up for in sparks.

In the fourth or fifth grade, I go on a school field trip to Sutter's Fort. My friend Carrie has given me a bandana cut into fringe and decorated with pony beads for my birthday. I wear it around my neck on the field trip. When I spin around, it swings away from me. When I stop spinning it lands on my chest like a breastplate. In the pictures from that day, my classmates crowd around each other, hamming it up for the camera. There are pictures that show me smiling.

Me, my classmates, and anyone who grew up along Highway 49 in the foothills of the Sierra Nevada are taught from a young age about the value of gold. We may not understand it, but when we scrub ourselves clean, the bathtub is ringed with gold at the waterline. We come out of the womb as alchemists. I can't remember a time when I wasn't trying to become someone else.

∞

A gold rush has a particular life cycle. The start of a gold rush is often birthed by the discovery of gold by an individual. A la James Marshall in the river.

Placer mining is the mining of a stream bed, the sorting and sifting and separating of alluvium in the search for gold, all the while one's hands turning wrinkled, waterlogged skin coming loose and swilling downstream. Panning for gold is a search for something precious. This search eventually evolves. Once a placer miner realizes that there is more gold to capture, the placer miner ups the ante with sluice boxes, hydraulic mining, diversions, dams, tunnels, and dredging. And then there's hard rock mining—excavation of the mother lode.

A mother lode is a major vein of gold ore. Placer miners perhaps follow the gold upstream until they discover the source. They perhaps realize that this glittering cleave in the earth is what sends nuggets and flakes sparking downstream. The little pot of gold at the start of the river rainbow. When people talk about a motherlode, they are talking about gold, but they are also talking about the birthplace of something valuable, real or imaginary. You, like me, might ask yourself *what is the difference?*

You might find it surprising that some think gold was produced in supernova nucleosynthesis or in the collision of neutron stars. If this is the case, then gold—dense and heavy—has sunk toward the earth's center. If this is the case, this is not the exact gold we are sluicing and sifting and digging for near the surface of the land. Prospectors in the California Gold Rush were searching for a more youthful gold spit out by underwater sea volcanoes four hundred million years ago and eventually carried down the steep of the mountains that vaulted upward from the ancient seafloor.

You might find it surprising that gold is quite soft and malleable. It can be reshaped, hammered to a thin, nearly-transparent sheet. You can eat it, and probably have, flakes flecking the top of some chocolate dessert.

I understand the aesthetic value of gold and am willing to assume that most humans—like most magpies—like shiny things. Flakes have been found in Paleolithic caves. Egyptians topped their pyramids with gold. Romans covered their ceilings in gold. Aztecs had gold in great abundance (excrement of the gods) until Spain stole it. Humans have long gilded gold leaf or gold powder to other materials (wood, stone, metal) to create the illusion that a thing is entirely made of gold. And, chances are, if you have anything made of gold, it comes from the South African gold belt where the deepest mine in the world—a 90-minute elevator ride in a shaft 2 ½ miles straight down—moves past geologic layers that hold the history of dinosaurs to unearth gold.

Gold is beautiful, scarce, and offers prized physical characteristics unique to a metal. These qualities contribute to its value. Still, I can't help but wonder what we have missed in our desperate search for gold. With our eyes peeled for sparks, for light glinting perpendicular, what aren't we seeing?

∞

There are old mine shafts all around the place where I grew up. When the ranchers come across one, they put up a fence to avoid losing cattle. Around there, property lines are marked with barbed wire fences. This same barbed wiring fencing—or maybe even hog wire fencing with its tidy quadrants of protection—might be put up around old mine shafts.

A mineshaft is a hole in the ground. A mineshaft is a narrow hole pointed steeply down. As kids, we throw rocks down the hole to see how deep it is. Shale on shale is a sharp sound. Shale on dirt is dull and full of ache. The wind has been knocked clean out of the throw. If you scream into a mineshaft, the scream will be swallowed.

A mineshaft is a vertical portal to what lies beneath. It is a place that has been excavated for the sole purpose of accessing further excavation sites. The hills around the place where I grew up are honeycombed with old mineshafts and tunnels. Earlier this fall, my dad sends a text with a picture of a hole in the ground. The hole is surrounded by new winter grass growing over browned summer grass. *What is it?* I ask him. The ground has caved in over an old mining tunnel. Soon, someone will come by and put a fence around the hole.

According to the Oxford Dictionary, "speculation" is "the forming of a theory or conjecture without firm evidence." According to the Oxford Dictionary, "speculation" is "investment in stocks, property, etc. in the hope of gain but with the risk of loss." Both of the words "prospect" and "speculate" stem, at least in part, from the Latin specere, *to look*. I think about this after I ask a friend for his opinion on a one-sentence bio I need to write. I come up with *XXX is a prose writer born in Gold Country destined for speculation*, and he asks if my readers will mine me. Mining and alchemy, and prospecting are endeavors that carry an inherent risk. *Looking* carries an inherent risk. It would be safer not to look. It has been safer for me not to look.

This is how I tell real gold from fool's gold: the former has soft edges, and the latter has sharp, square edges. Pyrite, aka fool's gold, is what I search for every time I cross a vein of milky quartz rock on trails near where I grew up. I am always looking down, waiting for the light to catch. Pyrite is what my dad and I pry loose from rock bed and tuck into our pockets. We do this at the old Gold Cliff mine pit near the house where I grew up. I feel—just a little—like I am Indiana Jones, hunting for the holy grail. To prospect is to seek. Playing prospector comes naturally to me, even if I am searching for a proxy.

My friend asks if I am looking out into the distance and privately wanting to be discovered. He asks this because I am a mystery to him, and he wonders if I am a mystery to my readers. My writing is like a strip tease because my living is like a strip tease. I am a mystery. I can't remember a time when I wasn't trying to become someone.

∞

When I stand at the edge of a mineshaft with the sun at my back, my shadow plunges partway inside. It's dangerous, I'm told, to go into old mineshafts, so I don't. Tunnels could collapse. The air could be toxic to my oxygen-hungry lungs. Still, the possibility of what a descent might reveal is electrifying.

The summer before I moved from the Sierra Nevada mountains to the Cascade Range, I became obsessed with the idea of finding a crystal cave that I've heard locals talk about for years. Imagine this: a cave big enough to stand in and walk around in. Imagine this cave covered in crystals jutting their sharp, clear geometry across every surface. I can't imagine anything more beautiful. The fact that it is hidden is the cherry on top.

The cave's general location is on the eastern side of the highest point of the mountain pass, where the western flank gives way to the east, near the spot where an impressive stand of aspen trees light up yellow every autumn. I go to this spot and look around. I see an old cabin, an old mining cart, and bits of metal trash crusted with rust. I walk a road that crosses vein after vein of dark-hued rocks growing lawns of tiny crystals. This seems like a promising sign.

I am interested in holes. I am interested in the gaps in what I seem to know and not know about myself, in what I can and cannot remember. What can be discovered in the absence? I speculate. I make up plausible stories based on what isn't there. I come to know the blank space by its shape. What could have made such a shape?

I am looking for markers—quartz veins—so I know where to dig. I am looking for gold—I can't help myself. But I am learning to look for other things, too. I am building my histories out of the space left after excavation.

I return more than once to try and find the crystal cave. I take others along to help. I show them the old cabin, the rusted mine cart, and even an old viewpoint marked rimmed by a rock wall but no crystal cave.

∞

When I am asked to recall something or to remember, I freeze. I shift into a solid state, and memories cease to lap at my feet. When I am asked to imagine, I surrender. I can play at this. I can create blanks to fill in and then fill in those blanks. Like John Marshall, I am leaning over the channel below his mill, dipping my hand into the water. I am in a dreamy state of mind. I watch skeeter bugs skim along the water's surface and send small oak branches downstream on their maiden voyage.

Discovery lacks volition. Mining is a search for something specific. To lean into eureka, then, perhaps means an initial willingness to come to the water's edge.

Toward the end of the summer, I run into a neighbor. We stand on granite, and the sun is peaked overhead. He tells me that the crystal cave was actually an old mineshaft and that the mineshaft has since been filled in. I think about the old mine cart, the rusted metal lying about. There had been a hole, and the hole had been filled in entirely.

∞

I am trying to remember. My therapist has asked me to start at the beginning, and we have. From conception to the gestation period to my birth. *What was it like in your mother's womb?* she asks. Some people can remember this... a feeling, a sensation in their body. I am not one of those people. *Dark?* I say. I have come to therapy for many reasons, chief among them that I would like to remember more about myself. It hasn't been working. I can't remember a time...

Another day, Kim asked me to visualize my birth and to imagine my adult self interacting with my youngest self. This is how I learned that I was born from the earth and swaddled in the blades of tall grasses. I am born calm. As a newborn, I lie still in a hollow on a hillside—tall green grasses, vines, trees. It is bright, protected, and fertile. A dark grey wolf watches over me.

What I'm telling you isn't true. But what I'm telling you isn't *not true* either. Where there are blanks, I trust the vivid, knee-jerk speculative process to render the truth in a way that cannot be ignored.

> This is why I've asked you here.
> To stand near the edge with me.
> How deep do you think it is?

3

A Bird Knocking Again and Again on a Window

When I was little and stayed at my grandmother's house, I would wake up in the middle of the night because my grandmother was awake. Sometimes crying. Sometimes cleaning. Sometimes working urgently on a project. I could hear her in other parts of the house or see light pushing its way beneath the door of the spare bedroom where I slept. I remember thinking that the sound of her, awake and pulsing—a bird knocking again and again on a window—was the loneliest sound in the world. I felt all the lonelier for being the one to hear it.

My grandmother sewed sachets and other things. She filled these little packets with lavender or scented them with strawberry oil and tucked them into drawers with underwear, socks, or shirts. I still have tiny bundles of lavender I've brought with me from house to house, dresser drawer to dresser drawer. The scent is long gone.

Once, my grandmother got the idea to make pillows filled with plastic bags. When I put my ear against these pillows, I could hear a hundred bags settling and crinkling—a thousand tiny bird heartbeats and a million slight wing adjustments.

When I was 15, I stopped going to school halfway through the year. It was an El Niño year, and the rains had come suddenly and heavily. Hillsides slid away, tearing out hundred-year-old pines. An invisible leak in the car made for a half-inch of water on the floorboard. Things were not as they'd always seemed. The ground couldn't hold me. And when it rained, the worms rose up from their flooded homes and crawled onto the sidewalks of my high school. Waterlogged worms were bulging on the overcast gray cement all over campus. I was careful to step around them. But this was before I decided to stop going to school. Then I stopped going.

She was born too soon, my mother says of my grandmother. Prematurely. Her nerve endings didn't fully develop. They didn't have a chance. Or she didn't have a chance.

I consider this story as I watch the robins overwhelm the tree outside my window.

Recently, the robins have taken over my town, keening from tree to tree, eating winter berries, and congregating for warmth. There hasn't been this much snow in decades, the locals say. I've been here 11 months, and the mob of robins seems to portend something important, though a write-up in the paper explains they come every year. It also says they can get drunk from eating fermented berries.

She was born too soon. I consider this story of my grandmother. When a mother talks about her own mother's birth, is it a reverse birth story? A just-so story? Does it explain certain things about her, or does it explain things about us—the family? Or perhaps it explains how we are able to, but also cannot, love in my family? Is it a divination?

Sometimes, the robins seem violent in their mass joy.

Sometimes, their shrieks fall onto my ears like foreboding.

The robins have migrated from the north, looking for water and juniper berries. They'll leave in a couple weeks. They'll look for mates with an instinct for spring. They'll get territorial. They'll have babies. They'll eat their fill of fermented berries, and when the ground begins to thaw, they'll search for earthworms by cocking their heads to the side, using one eye and then the other to scan the ground.

When I was 15, I stopped going to school. This was the first time depression bloated me with gray. No longer would I spend my days walking around campus with a blue plaid blanket wrapped around me. I slipped instead into the deep blue sea of my bedroom. Feeling like the tea leaves clumped at the bottom of a porcelain teacup or a stunted lifeline on the palm of a hand.

To imagine a future, one must be able to call a past to mind. Suddenly, I remembered nothing.

When I was 17, I stopped going to school. Again, when I was 19 and then 20. I was a good student. I still got my work done. Time was still measured in semesters and quarters and credits and grades. Somnambulant and bleary-eyed, I somehow dotted i's, crossed t's.

My grandmother moved into my family home when I was in high school. She had dementia. She was pleasant. The forgetting had stripped away the sadness that made her nocturnal. The forgetting made her more accepting of the world around her. One morning, she came into my bedroom confused by the diaper on her body. She was calm. She was looking for help. An explanation. It was more than I knew how to give. I pretended to be asleep. Played dead.

And when my mother said of my grandmother that her nerve endings hadn't fully developed, she was saying that my grandmother felt too much. That she went out in the world feelings first, vulnerable, raw, exposed. That this might explain her in a way nothing else could.

Sometimes, my grandmother would spray-paint the step from the kitchen to the garage a bright orange. So people wouldn't forget it was there and fall.

Sometimes, my grandmother would snap the rubber bands around her wrist, reminding her of something she needed to do that day. Because, in a pinch, pain will help us remember.

What other ways of being have I learned from her?

Sometimes my grandmother held me close enough that I felt the bristle of her upper lip against my cheek. She would hum to herself and make us dinner. I would lose time looking at each button in the overflowing metal tin in her sewing room.

When my grandmother dies, I am the only one not in the hospital. Is this true? Or is this a just-so story I tell myself? A story that describes how a person who looks just like me must continue to play dead? Lie fallow. Lie in wait while the living are dying, while the ground is frozen beneath the low angle of the sun.

All last week, I went to work from 8 a.m. to 5 p.m. Then I came home and lay in bed from 6 p.m. to 6 a.m. I am in hiding again. Time is measured in hours, by a workday, by years alive, and by the snow piling up outside my window and the number of consecutive days it has been below freezing. It is winter. I forget, then I remember.

The upstairs loft in this house is where I write. Last summer, I angled and lowered the blind pull to raise the slats and let light in over my desk. Another dead bird on the roof. It must be how the light reflects off the window, showing a path where there is only obstacle. There is something to this, I think. Something to there being another dead bird on the roof. There is something to only being able to look at things peripherally, singularly, twisting from side to side, craning for the sight of a worm. I worry I don't know how to see what it is. I worry—now that the tilt of earth's axis has brought me back to winter, to the beauty and the monotony of the white landscape, the snow piling up—that I will go dormant, waiting for the spring melt.

4

Notes on Water

I remember going out into the rain. I put on extra layers and saw they would get good and soaked through. The rain called to me, and I walked between the rows of fruit trees with the base of their trunks painted white. Sometimes a person doesn't know if they're dreaming or awake unless they are wet, unless they leave a puddle on the linoleum when they do go back inside.

Remembering seems sad. I am sad for the little girl standing in the rain. Not because of the rain. But because often she has to stand in the not-rain. Because she often finds herself dry and steaming in a patch of sun.

Is the loneliness of being a child linear, or is it the present—dervish—tasselling backward and forward?

Perhaps the sacred is what's missing. Perhaps I need to walk barefoot and feel the bite of the land.

Today, in the bath, I felt the water lapping against my thigh as though feeling for the first time. In movement is pleasure. In the lapping and the licking and the rub and the surge. I lift my legs out of the water and then submerge them. Repeat. As the water surrounds and falls away, surrounds and falls away. This is how I trace myself. I make a map of my body out of water. It feels like a place I might like to want to live one day.

5

What Shape a Memory Should Take

When J and I carpool to Portland to meet our friends to catch a plane to Washington, D.C., for the Women's March, she tells me that she feels as though everything she does has ripple effects. She feels her every action matters. *Not me,* I say. I have a history of feeling unsubstantial.

We cross over the Cascades, dropping from the high desert into and out of a river canyon, skirting Mt. Hood, eventually holding parallel to the Columbia River. Somewhere along this river, the nuclear production complex that yielded plutonium for the Manhattan Project sprawls, now mostly decommissioned. The last time I came this way, with another friend, she asked me how much money she'd have to give me to swim in the river. It looked dirty to her. It was summer then, and I looked across the water toward beach chairs and umbrellas spread across sandy rises. *Nothing,* I said. *This is a river safe for swimming.*

What does mostly decommissioned mean anyway? Later, I look it up. The weapons production reactors were decommissioned at the end of the Cold War, but there was still the issue of waste: millions of gallons of radioactive and solid waste, along with contaminated groundwater. When I bring it up on a map, I see that it is located 200-plus miles upstream from Portland. I see that it is now a National Park. I see that I can visit, can take a tour if I like.

Tell me more about feeling insignificant, J says. I wonder if it would be a relief for her if I could convince her to also feel this way. *I think that everything I do makes a difference,* she says again. She nods toward the river and tells me that a boy she knows jumped into a group of baby water moccasins. He barely lived. She still wants an answer from me. I don't have one. She wants to know who I am. If I could, I would tell her that humans are

60-70% water, which is to say, I can't imagine that what creates us might also kill us.

This isn't entirely true. I know that anything can kill us. I know that everything can kill us. I know that, most often, the cause of death is just the final straw. Later, I find out that there are no water moccasins in the Columbia River. This calls everything into question: J's memory and my credibility. Still, I live in fear of what I cannot see, of something upstream being drawn toward me, of what lies beneath the surface.

On the night of the 2016 presidential election—two and a half months prior—I am at a poetry event in a church that has been repurposed as a venue for community events. Swatches of yellow and orange textured glass fill half of a wall. The glass has tiny cuts like the feathery fractal pattern of ice I've seen on my windshield on cold mornings. I can't see where we're going, I think to myself, seated on a pew that runs along the sidewall of the building. The poet is on stage to my right and has asked us to turn off our cell phones. I want to know the polling results. I want to watch the states turn red and blue. In an adjacent room, someone gasps, and I know that something terrible is happening outside the room where the poet talks about revenge dreams. When I look at the glass swatches, I try to remember if it's raining outside. Rain seems to portend a certain kind of fate.

The day after the Women's March, we walked from the Korean War Memorial to the World War II Memorial, monument to monument, through darkness and drizzle. I've never been here, and it feels important. Akin to making a National Park out of a decommissioned nuclear production complex, the monuments are constructed of a complicated past. Marble and stone, and bronze urge us not to forget. There is so much to remember. Too much. And though I appreciate the heft and solidity of a monument, I don't like being told what shape a memory should take.

For example, I remember that at the Lincoln Memorial, a young woman asks me to take a picture of her. Her phone rings while I'm holding it; she takes the call; I wonder if I have to wait for her to finish the conversation; I wonder if I'm still responsible for commemorating her visit.

At the Lincoln Memorial, a young man asks a young woman to marry him. The crowd cheers when she says yes. Because the couple is behind me, the cheers startle me, and I bolt out of the crowd and onto the stairs. We are all here for different reasons.

At the Lincoln Memorial, a stage and risers sit empty. Washington, D.C., is still set up for the inauguration. Chairs in rows on the West Lawn. Temporary flooring, fencing, and barricades on The Mall and in the streets. Some of the portable toilets are padlocked. They were for use only by inauguration-goers. It is misty and damp. A little otherworldly. A little like a theme park after hours.

Here's the thing about traumatic memories. They are stored in your body like separate entities—jars of river water collected from all over the West—sitting next to each other in the fridge, not touching, kept cool so life cannot grow. These memories-in-isolation don't interact with other memories-in-isolation; they are each a part of a larger story that can't be told. When J asks me to tell her about feeling insignificant, I list the things I can't remember. This calls everything into question. I am convinced of my forgetfulness even when there is evidence to the contrary.

On the night of the 2016 presidential election, the poet says that talking about an experience or memory changes it and creates a new experience.

On the night of the 2016 presidential election, the poet says that nothing on our planet is affected more than water.

These things are said at different points in the evening. These things are said before, during, and after the poet also says, *it's just like me to forget where Venus is*, and *when a species leaves a planet, they take their sounds with them*, and *creativity will keep you alive in ways you can't imagine.*

Days after the election, we booked our flights to Washington, D.C. When the time comes, we go from one coast to another, crossing over river after river after river until, finally, we cross over the Anacostia. We march. And the next day, we visit the monuments in the darkness and the drizzle, and I think about the stories they tell. Stories erected to a collective memory-keeping. Stories erected in collective memory-creation.

Here's the thing about memory. Memory and story change over time, winding toward a coherent narrative that also changes over time. Researchers say that our minds make happy stories. Except that, traumatic memories don't change over time; they don't integrate, and they don't shift toward happiness. If happiness were made into a monument, what would it look like? And these monuments, so many of them erected to remind us of traumatic events, what has been lost. . . What does this mean for our sense of ourselves as a whole?

On the flight back from Washington D.C. I am suddenly reminded of a trip I took long ago to a music festival in Las Vegas. I take out this memory and consider it. I change it through the mere act of remembering. I put it back. I wonder if I will forget this trip in time and what it will look like when I take it out and remember it again. As usual, I confuse remembering with forgetting and equate remembering with safety.

For reasons unknown to me, I could not take the only empty seat on the Metro the night before. I was tired. I wanted to rest. The empty seat was next to a stranger, a young man slouching in his seat, listening to music, waiting for his stop. I stood, knowing I was scared, without knowing why. But here's the thing. I knew why. When I say things like *I don't know* or *I can't remember* what I really mean is, *I won't.* I didn't want to feel my substance in the way that sitting next to a stranger would make me feel my substance. In a way, I felt mostly decommissioned, my senses pulled from the present to focus instead on waste held in underground storage. Things out of sight.

How could it be possible, I think to myself, to forget this weekend? Millions of people. Moment in history. Unforgettable.

We take an Uber from the Portland airport back to our friend's place, loading our bags into J's car and starting the three-hour drive over the mountains. This is what happened yesterday. I repeat the events silently to myself as J and I drive back over the mountains, homeward. We pass through forests and over roads gritty with cinder rock. I go over the events again and again, but I'm sure I'll remember it wrong or remember all the wrong things.

This is what it looks like to try and build a monument of your life: holding water in cupped hands.

Many years ago, I was at the place where the Columbia River meets the Pacific Ocean. I stood at a high point and looked down. I felt akimbo on the edge of time, a confluence of what was, what is, what might be. I asked to speak to any ghosts who might be present, but I got no replies. In retrospect, I wonder about the river water, forging its sinuous path from the Rocky Mountains to the Pacific, past violent and contaminated histories. It must take an ocean to hold all of that.

6

Relic Radiation

I want to know about the Big Bang. Expansion, explosion, evolution. Scientists know what happened milliseconds *after* the Big Bang. There are ideas and a growing consensus about what happened *before.* It's without certainty, though… that *bang* moment.

I want to know what happened in the *bang* moment.

At the National Museum of Natural History, I see star stuff. Ancient stardust that traveled to Earth inside a meteorite named Allende in 1969. It is older than our solar system. This star stuff resembles fine, white sand and is housed inside a small vial behind a magnifying glass: tiny diamonds born from a dying star. It is the Monday of a holiday weekend at the National Museum of Natural History. It is crowded and loud with parents and children and tourists like me. I wait until the magnifying glass is open and look closely at the star stuff. It looks like a concoction I might have made as a kid: flour and confectioner's sugar, water, and some of my mom's perfume. I can't help but be swayed by its presence. It is tangible. I can almost touch it.

Scientists study the universe's evolution via relic radiation, known as the cosmic microwave background. The "cosmic microwave background light is a traveler from far away and long ago. When it arrives, it tells us about the whole history of our universe." What's coming through now is from a period likened to the Dark Ages. Ordinary matter—the kind that coalesces to form stars and planets and us—was surrounded by dark matter during this time, and dark matter doesn't emit light.

We can't see it. We can't directly observe it. But, dark matter created the structure for ordinary matter to clump and evolve. Ordinary matter like the ancient stardust I saw at the National Museum of Natural History. Ordinary matter like me.

Sometimes, when I was young, I would stare into the mirror, wondering if the reflection beyond could be trusted.

Sometimes I would hear sirens in the distance. If I was home alone, kneeling on the couch, possibly feeling lonely, and looking out the window, I might wonder if they were for me and what I'd done wrong.

I am comprised of ordinary matter. But I am also comprised of something intangible or, at least, something I don't yet have the instruments to measure.

Physicist and cosmologist Lisa Randall doesn't want us to confuse dark matter with something ominous. In her book *Dark Matter and the Dinosaurs*, she likens it "to entities that remain unnoticed but influence the workings of the world," but the "dark" in its name should not be appropriated to mean anything dire or frightening.

Still, I might wonder if the sirens were for me. The sense that I was wrong, had done wrong, formed a cocoon around everything else. I was afraid.

Dark matter constitutes about 85% of the stuff of the universe. Since it doesn't emit light (astronomy is the study of light that reaches Earth), scientists study dark matter's effects (gravitational yee and yaw) on brighter matter.

I am worried that I can't recall my first memory. I am worried that I don't know if certain things I liken to memory are real, or invented, or swiped from 3 x 5 pictures taken of me when I was young. I wonder why the memories that sneak through are important. Or not. This is what a friend has to say about writing nonfiction: *it's almost cooler to explore why memories are recalled than talking about the memories themselves.*

She's right. I'm missing the point when I say: I am obsessed with what I don't know. Perhaps, it's more interesting to consider *how* I don't know. Perhaps instruments of measurement can be developed for *how.*

You're still finding yourself, the psychic says, *and your intuition is very strong.* We sit across from one another, a glass coffee table in between. Her space is on the second story of a 1970s office building; the walls are wood paneling, and the windows are single pane. A crystal ball sits on a shelf. *You don't need me,* she says. *You are your own oracle,* she says.

How you do anything is how you do everything, the teacher says. He sits in a wood-backed chair with striped cushions. I sit at a table, on a bench. He asks me to anticipate what's coming next, what I will do, think, feel. *You know yourself best,* he says. I think about the last time I was in class with him and come up with an idea of who I will be in the next hour. At the end of class, he'll say, *You aren't the same person you were when we started.*

Ancient light. The light from the cosmic microwave background is from billions of years ago. Scientists study it, learning about the entire history of the cosmos in the process. But they also study how the journey changes it.

I recently learned about a new framework for looking at emotions researched by Lisa Feldman Barrett. Emotions are not innate, nor are they universal. They are culturally specific. And individuals express them differently. This is why a friend of mine laughs when she's afraid. For each emotion we might think of as inherently human, a culture exists that doesn't have it. To grossly simplify: emotions construct my world. Emotions are built based on nuanced sensory feedback, available concepts, and experience.

From the Latin *oraculum, orare* means *speak.* An oracle is the message. Once, I would have interpreted message to mean the *bang* moment. Now, I am more interested in *how* the message comes through. If I am stardust, ordinary matter, and light coming to Earth, and if I am interested in learning of and from the dark matter that I cannot see, I must turn my attention toward *how* the dark matter twists and bends the light.

7

High Place Phenomenon

High place phenomenon is the feeling you get when standing on a bridge or a cliff or the overlook at the Grand Canyon or rounding the corner of an alpine pass. A flicker of an urge to jump.

This is not to be mistaken for a suicidal inclination. This flicker lives outside of the desire of wanting to die, and, in fact, it may have more to do with wanting to live. The urge might just be the body misinterpreting a safety signal. Or cognitive dissonance. After all, we are better at guessing horizontal distances than vertical heights. And then there is the kind of flying that we do when we are dreaming. And the story of Icarus that has been gliding around our collective consciousness for centuries.

Do you remember Sartre's discussion of vertigo? We, humans, are "also an object in the world, subject to gravitation..."

Sometimes, it is difficult to stay afloat when I am flying in my dream. I seem to lack buoyancy, or the buoyancy that I start with deflates with my growing realization that I can fly—am flying!—and soon my toes are trilling through water if there is water or pushing off land if there is land. Dream logic seems to posit that I can fly if I don't question it. As if the questioning were the sun's heat melting my dreamy wax wings.

In "Being and Nothingness," Sartre continues: "Vertigo is anguish to the extent that I am afraid not of falling over the precipice, but of throwing myself over." Or, as Emily Dickinson wrote, "'Hope' is the thing with feathers." This flash—the flicker of an urge to jump—could be an expression of possibility.

Gravity invited gaseous matter to coalesce into stars which further clustered into galaxies, including our own. On Earth, gravity grounds us and gives weight to rocks, park benches, persimmons, gondolas, and steaming hot mugs of chai. The moon's gravity produces ocean tides. And yet gravity is the weakest of the four fundamental forces of physics. My acceptance of gravity doesn't negate this urge to jump primarily because this urge doesn't come from the prefrontal cortex. This urge doesn't exist in logic.

If I am honest, I think there is more to this phenomenon than an urge, whether biological, existential, or mythical. How can I not be moved by high places? Every hole has a rim. By its very nature, a hole is defined, in part, by a surrounding high place.

As a child, I have a recurring dream. I am in a large building where several floors surround an open center. There is a lot of wood and an air of invention to the place, as if industrious makers tinker and make headway toward epiphanies during the day. At night, the place is mine. If I am on one of the top floors, I can push myself over the balcony to fly. In other dreams in other places, I need to get a running start. And even then, even after sprinting across a hillside downy with green, I might never leave the ground.

I can't say for certain, but I'm willing to venture a guess. A hole is a place I can jump into.

8

Hole Series

The Hole or An Introduction

Surrounded by Douglas Fir and on a road flanked by persistent red cinder rock, we drive toward the lake, which is round and vibrant, an eye in the wilderness.

Me: There's so much I don't remember. And I don't always trust what I do remember. There are holes.

Arielle: Write about the hole.

Me: Worse, there is the fear that there is no hole.

Arielle: Write about the fear.

Later Aisha brings out watercolors, and I paint a storyboard of the hole. There are four frames.

In the first, the house that my parents built—where I grew up—sits on its idyllic hill. The house opens on a center hinge like a dollhouse in the second frame. There is a small black blob. By the fourth frame, the hole takes up all of the space.

v. 1 or Here's What I Know

There are holes.

When the gears of my memory glut for flight, there are holes. I have been terrified to find out what who I've become has been through.

At EMDR, I take the devices in my hands. The pulse is passed back and forth and left to right, and I remember something. I remember reading something somewhere about integration, how important it is to crawl as a baby, to have the opposite parts of your body working in unison. How you shouldn't skip this step.

So, I guess when I say I can't remember anything, it's a lie. There are holes.

Or one hole?

Am I a sedimentary landscape?

Scientists can point to the K-Pg layer—a thin band of clay—as the time when the asteroid hit the earth. In the big scheme, this accuracy seems miraculous. Perhaps my memory is more geologic.

Perhaps my cavities are canyons, sandstone worn by a river. Perhaps my torso, limbs, and face are talus from the patient, but certain, progress of glacier. Perhaps my memories are jarred and jumbled by my shifting tectonic plates.

I remember what it means to be absent. And what is a hole if not absent? It defines what isn't.

v. 2 or What I Don't Remember

I don't remember how I came to be here, terrified. I approach the hole. I tiptoe to the hole like a dog trying to sneak up on a cat. The hole has quick reflexes. Which is to say that it is more agile than it looks.

It rumbles awake and stretches. I bring binoculars to my eyes. I see it, squirming around like a virus in a petri dish. I walk toward it, but it's already gone.

What I want most.

What I mean when I say "hole" is void, but also fear, but also hope.

v. 3 or i walk up to the edge of the hole

i wonder if I'm going to
          jump

sometimes my muscles itch for leap
something to do with birth
or unreliable impulse control
something about the metaphor of being buried alive even if ideas are just-so stories
something about coming out the other
          side

around here
ranchers put fences around holes in the ground
so the cows don't fall in
don't get too close to
the edge

i'm told
time and time
again, sometimes
i
send things into
the hole
a rock or
a prayer

if by prayer you mean
something akin to hope, something akin to
uncertainty
something akin to an opening

if by an opening you mean to say

how little you remember
how the hole came to be both is and is not a mystery
this town was carved by miners

sometimes, we stand inside a hole that is a square footprint
stamped
always someone has been before you

we bring buckets
and use small hand tools
to pry loose
that which glitters

v. 4 or Tsk

A shame—still, she asks
Who will fight for you if not you?

The first time I felt shame was today. The bright of it. It was also the thousandth time. The billionth. This is the way with shame: likewise familiar and foreign. Both stardust and epidermis. At least, this is where I feel it most… deep in the starry recesses (call it gravity) of me, one celestial body collides with another, and there is nothing. Nothing nothing. A void like a rip in the fabric of the universe, nothing.

Nothing to do but draw a line of its trajectory across my thigh.

Today, shame feeds me grapes one by one by one. Once upon a time, I lay under a lattice overgrown with Thompson Seedless grapes: this is how I know I am wrong. And so my story is the story of my parents and the story of theirs. To think that the shame I carry could have traveled from Prussia. Sicily is a rock being kicked by the dainty boot of the mainland. Is this the reason we don't mourn ourselves?

.
.
.
.
.
.
.
.
.
.
.
.
.
.

Today, the shame. The air isn't mine. People, not mine. The sun. Nothing is mine. Nothing to do but draw a line of nothing across my thigh. There is blood. My body is my Lascaux, my place of reckoning recollections of the hunt.

v. 5 >>>>> or My Sister Texts

My sister texts to say that a plumber is coming to look at the shower drain. We live together. Cool. I say I didn't know there was anything wrong with it.

And just that morning, I awoke and stood leaning into the light, gradually saturating and feeling around for my life.

My sister texts to say that a plumber is coming to look at the shower drain. Just FYI. It will be fixed soon. Fixed? I'll write back. What's wrong with it? I think about all the times our father had to use a snake to retrieve monsters of clumped and dissolving hair from the pipes.

My sister texts to say that a plumber is coming to look at the shower drain. Why? I ask. She tells me about the standing water. She tells me how it won't go down. She tells me that we have a problem.

I always take the first shower. I move a washcloth across my body. I come to, leaning against the wall, water pelting my stomach.

My sister texts to say that a plumber is coming to look at the shower drain. She's tried everything. Drano, baking soda, vinegar, suction, fury. We need a professional.

She wonders how I didn't notice that I was ankle-deep in standing water that morning.

Thanks for taking care of it, I say. I take a deep breath and continue to swim.

v. 6 or One Voice in the Dark Says to Another

Voice in the dark *what are you afraid of?*

No reply. Darkness and somewhere far off the sound of water dripping into itself.

It has been like this for an eternity, for eons, for a blink of the magma pupil at the earth's center. It has been dark until it isn't. And always, the water is dripping into itself, coursing over rock toward its likeness. When we are born, it is from the water. When we are born, it is from the rock. We are enclosure upon enclosure of water and minerals that grow up to be voices in the dark. In some ways, we are sedimentary.

One voice in the dark says to another voice in the dark *I know you can hear me.*

Drip. Drip. Water unto water.

I can hear you, but I can't see you.

So what says one voice in the dark.

Darkness continues to stuff steel wool into the cracks. It keeps out the mice and the light.

What are you afraid of one voice in the dark asks again.

Everything.

Come on.

Everything.

Outside of the darkness, swiftness and industry and the spin drag of gravity that pins the light-walkers out from under the dark ruffles off sleep and shakes self into day.

One voice in the dark says to another voice in the dark *I am afraid I've been sorely mistaken.*

There is a stifled banging coming from outside the darkness. Light-walkers dropped something.

I'm afraid that I've looked and seen nothing where there was simply nothing to see.

v. 7 or Not That I Even Want to Share a Sentence with Columbus

But he took himself
so seriously, didn't he.
And what a
mistake to
make.
The only god
worth kneeling
before is the
god of
arbitrariness.
Who, as
everyone
knows,
encapsulates
all possibilities and all
possible identities but who
kind of shrugs at it all. As if to say.
Whatever you do next doesn't matter.

But it matters, Columbus. It matters, god of arbitrariness.

Because a word like discover is a way to talk about something that's always been there. To discover, then, is to admit you're ignorant.

One would think said discoverer might want to be low-key about it all.

His eyes had been made of clay. Columbus' eyes were hand-formed in Genoa. One was named Isabella, and the other was Ophelia.

The god of arbitrariness thinks they are being misrepresented. They want to talk about what it means when they shrug. It means one thing is another, and both are nothing and everything. You see?

It means truth is not a fixed point.
It means that there is nowhere to go from here but anywhere.

9

Bury

Her grandfather killed himself on a Friday. Don't worry, he'd said sometime the week prior; I'll wait until after Thanksgiving. Not about to ruin your holiday. Did you know the right lung has three lobes and the left has two? As if sheer lack of symmetry will make a person sick. As if an unbalanced equation is what does you in in the end. Because, you see, he had cancer in that third lobe. The inferior lobe. Goes without saying.

The doctors found it late, and he didn't want to do the whole chemo/radiation thing. He wasn't one to grow weak in front of other people. The whole wearing-a-hospital-gown and lying-in-a-hospital-bed and eating-from-a-hospital-tray and dying-in-a-hospital-room thing wasn't for him.

So it was to be a gun to the head.

Sometime the week prior, he is sipping Ensure through a straw. He's telling stories: the one where he's never had a cold a day in his life. The one where the docs say he has the knees of a forty-year-old. The one where life makes no sense because what you do (or don't do) often doesn't matter. Sometime that week, he tells her that he's going to die without her really knowing him, which, in a way, is hilarious. Downright laughable. From when she was a year old, she's lived right next door to him. Separated only by fields of natural grasses that greened, grew, bleached, and broke per the season, the occasional barbed wire fence, and acres of something ghostly and unknown, the kind of unknown that catches your breath and makes you curse, like when you lose earth and solid footing, like when your foot catches an unseen gopher hole, and you drop and midway down you understand it would be better to fall all the way in, but you won't fit, and you don't know how.

Her grandfather leaves his house on the Friday after Thanksgiving. She hears his truck as he drives past her house. She sits at the counter in the kitchen: cream tiles, square, grout the color of coffee with cream. This is the house that her parents built. She saw every part of it come together. And so it is this grout that she stares at, and maybe her hands, when she hears the truck mumble closer, then farther, like a sentence trailing off.

Eventually, a gunshot.

Eventually, she will walk onto the back deck and watch the sunset. She will walk to the spot on the hill behind the house where the black oaks grow, to see their yellows, to see their reds, to see some evidence that time hasn't stopped.

Otherwise, the forest is filled with the persistence of the live oaks, the bone-white spines of the white oaks. She will pick up a fallen red-orange leaf and bring it to her nose: the scent—sharp and pungent and sweet and decaying and courageous and scared—is the same sensation as the sound of air hollowing her own asymmetrical lobes. At some point, she will take a stick and dig. At some point, she will throw the stick aside and use her hands to ensure the hole is deep enough. At some point, she will bury the leaf. At some point, she will leave the dirt underneath her fingernails for days or maybe for a lifetime.

10

15.5 Paragraphs About Death

13. My grandmother lived without food and water for thirteen days while her children waited for her to die. She'd lived in a nursing home for eleven years, the inertia of not-knowing and un-being slow to gain mass. When she dies, we say things like "She wasn't herself," "What a blessing," and "We miss her" as we slip and gain traction between sadness and relief.

14. On the fourteenth day, I think about her death. I had nearly forgotten that she was still alive. Had she been? I hadn't seen her in years. No one should live like that.

93. My grandmother was 93 when she died. Or 91. Or 96. She was old, an age that might be better figured in the number of super moons witnessed, droughts, or earthquakes experienced. When you live to be that old, geological forces start to matter.

10. Ten days after my grandmother stopped taking food and water, I walked down a sidewalk in a town I'd just moved to, hundreds of miles from my grandmother and the rest of my family. It's barely mine. I barely belong. I walk carefully to avoid stepping in the goose poop that is everywhere. Back where I came from, I would kayak to a small granite island in the middle of an alpine lake and have the same problem. It might be that I share a migratory path with the Canadian geese.

49. When you come from a town that started as a California gold mining camp, the years between 1849 and 1949 are a little fuzzy. Purdyville was a small neighborhood in this town of Angels Camp where houses cleaved to the hillside. Bakers,

insurance salesmen, mechanics, and telephone repairmen tumbled out each morning. Nelson, a strongman covered in tattoos, lived there. My grandmother lived there as a girl. My father lived there as a boy. All the neighborhood children, including my dad, saw strongman Nelson's muscles, saw the epic poetry detailed there, and traced mud on their lanky limbs in biomimicry. At least, that's what I would have done if I were there.

11. I lived next to my grandparents as a toddler until I was elevn. They have a living room and a more formal living room. Sometimes, I sit alone in the more formal living room and look at the *Architectural Digests.* It is cool and dark and still in this room. It is quiet and empty in this room. I look at the pictures of fancy homes and wonder about the nature of want. In other words, I see things I think I should want.

37. Yet, here I am at age 37 without the narrative so many others have.

12. Twelve days after my grandmother stopped taking food and water, I curled up on my new mattress into the shape of a question mark. I am guilty of not knowing enough.

15. My grandmother was fifteen when she gave birth to her oldest son; my grandfather was maybe twenty. I place them in Purdyville soon after. If it's accusations we're after, her father was an alcoholic with yeast in his blood and yeast on his hands. Her mother was resilient—she hid (sometimes buried) coffee cans of cash, and she spoke in currencies of survival. If it's excuses we seek, then his mother was a shadow, and his father was an alcoholic in an arbiter's pastoral: black robe, wooden gavel.

49. If it's a metallurgical assay we're after, St. Sava Serbian Church sits on the western side of Purdyville, on the highway that stretches across time to the birthplace of pluck and desperation. The Italians—peasants—were few but tilled and

planted and picked most of the fruits and vegetables that made it to the tables in each dollhouse. The Irish and the Cornish had arrived first.

49. If it's smelting we use to extract, then we might look around to see that everyone was a claim jumper. The town is full of old mine shafts.

15. Fifteen days after my grandmother stopped taking food and water, two days after she died, I still feel guilty but also sad and compromised. She won't have a memorial, and my dad tells me he doesn't want one when his time comes. I am angry and sad and relieved. Are we a people who can't stand acknowledgment in life or death?

7. As a kid, my grandmother sang, "Here she comes, Miss America, " as I entered the room. She would feed me tri-colored Italian cookies and Neopolitan ice cream and let me watch The Mickey Mouse Club. We walked through open fields, and she let me go first, pretending I was a unicorn. We would walk to an old chimney, the only thing that remained from an old homestead. Roses grew around it and bloomed pale pink in the summer.

5. On the fifth day of the week, I am in my house when a neighbor peeks in through the window. I don't want to talk now. I learned this from my grandmother.

5.5 I am very good at hiding. My grandmother is gone; before she is gone, she is hidden inside confusion. I knit our confusion into knowing, a cowl that covers my throat, years (centuries) of opening our mouths and not knowing what to say.

11

Verse

So-and-so says so-and-so cried when she told her the story of the Greek myth: the one where the daughter is abducted, and the mother turns everything to winter. Another so-and-so's so-and-so asks me at dinner what I've been doing with my life. He doesn't mean it how it sounds; still, it sounds like the temperatures in my head are turning toward winter. I pass the butter when asked and agree that the tuna is cooked well and the sauce is perfect. This is how the years are measured. I smile at so-and-so and wonder when the snow will let up.

So-and-so thinks I'm younger than I am. He or she is far enough away from these furrows on my forehead. Or her or his sight isn't what it used to be. I answer so-and-so like this: in the garden of the house where I grew up, a small tree grew next to a gate on a path that led down the hill from the house. Near the roses, past the ginkgo. When you split into a pomegranate, another world opens up, seeds like a roe, like planets, garnet beads that stain like blood. I lick the so-and-so from my fingertips.

Persephone was swallowed into the underworld and stolen. Some call it an abduction, some a rape. Some might say she was innocent. There's always a piece of fruit when we talk about loss; in this case: a pomegranate; in this case: the fruit of the dead. If we just ignore the men in this story (boys will be boys, shrug it aside as locker room talk), know this: Persephone is the daughter of Demeter (who oversaw the harvest and the cycle of life and death). When Persephone was swallowed whole, Demeter let the earth go fallow, turning wholly, and instead, toward searching for her daughter. Winter came in her grief.

Here is the story of the word *verse.* It holds all of the seasons (except, maybe, for winter), and it is a hard worker. From the

Latin *versus.* A turn of the plow, a furrow. Verse is Demeter once again letting things grow. From above, these fields of corn artichokes, strawberries, almonds wheat show us that we will live.

When I write the word so-and-so, it means I can't remember. It means the kids are really not okay. It means to get back from the underworld; I need myth as my messenger. When I write the word Persephone, it means that I die at least once a year. When I return, I crush pomegranate seeds with a mortar and pestle. I add a thickening agent. When I write the word verse, it means I am trying.

12

Melancholy Woman

i.

A bruise is a blue thing. I give myself one when I somehow step on the lower edge of my bookshelf. I don't know how to manage it, but I keep the shelf from falling forward onto me and end up with a linear bruise on the arch of my foot. It appears the day after I fall foot first into the lower edge of my bookshelf, and I am pleased. A hurt made visible is a satisfying thing.

I returned to the bookshelf to remember what I had been looking for. These are books on my bookshelf with a blue spine: *Float* (Anne Carson), *The Chronology of Water* (Lidia Yuknavitch), *Days and Nights of Love and War* (Eduardo Galeano), *Lonely Planet Iceland*, Joan Didion's *Slouching Toward Bethlehem*, David James Duncan's *River Teeth* and *The Waves* (Virginia Woolf).

With my eyes closed, I open each page randomly and place my finger on a line.

A most beautiful sound[1]

I first met my mother the night before my first of three marriages when she turned to me and said, I almost married a rodeo man.[2]

I *didn't ask him why he didn't leave, so he wouldn't ask me why I didn't.*[3]

Do you see what I mean? Our interpretation is colored by intent. In this case, indigo stains my fingertips.

---

[1] Billie Holiday sings the blues.

[2] Something old, something new, something borrowed, something blue.

[3] If a ship's captain or an officer died while at sea, the crew would fly blue flags. When the ship returned to port, they would paint a blue band along its hull.

ii.

I am house-sitting, and I forget to bring my medication. I've missed two doses. But I've only missed two doses, I say to myself.

I take my medication at night, one and one-half pills. I take a pill between my teeth and bite in half. It's inexact, but so am I. When I take it, I get drowsy, which is why I take it at night. But it's true that I also feel more possible when I take it.

After missing two doses at work, I start crying at my desk. For no reason. I'm not certain that these two things are related, but I am not certain they are not. When I start to cry, I am inside a balloon. Its plastic stretched thin; I can see through its film of red to the outside—where everything is now tinged artificially rosy. I don't buy it for a second. I can touch it, but I know it isn't real.

Sadness is real. Sadness catches onto each breath and rides out of my lungs. Like a foxtail weed, determined to regenerate.

My coworker showed me permanent marker on his desktop where his son was coloring the night before. I give him a cleaner that will take it right off. When I move to the cupboard to put the cleaner back, I move slowly so as to not tip any sadness onto the carpet. Sadness is a deeper kind of stain.

Do you see what I mean?

This is what kills me about sadness. It is tinged with blue and lays a watery wash over everything. A blue balloon stretched over everything. A blue balloon stretched around me. Does this make *everything* blue, or does this make *me* blue?

iii.

"The caoutchouc is exceedingly elastic," Michael Faraday wrote in the Quarterly Journal of Science in 1824. Balloons were invented for myriad reasons, including military use and, like Faraday's intent, for use in scientific experiments. Galileo had even used a pig's bladder as some kind of proto-balloon in his lab to try and measure the weight of air. Whether balloons are filled with atmospheric air, the exhalation of breath, gases noble or ignoble, they exist to squeeze tight against what they stretch to hold. When they can't hold it any longer, a balloon will burst.

These are things people do with balloons: twist them into animal shapes, float in baskets beneath them, use them to treat arterial atherosclerosis, send them sounding into the sky to answer questions about the weather, and pop them for pornographic pleasure.

Do you understand that when I say balloon, I mean *something that stretches to accommodate*?

A yogi once told me that I breathe too shallowly, that we each have an allotted number of breaths to breathe in our lifetime, and that I was rushing my breathing and, therefore, shortening my life. Mostly, I remember that the yogi had a young daughter and a young wife who was pregnant with another. He seemed tired and unprepared for the earthly motions required by fatherhood. He seemed vaguely annoyed at all times. He struck me as someone not to be trusted to offer useful advice on how to exist in the physical plane, but I knew he was onto something about my breathing. I keep my breathing high and unattached, in and out and in and out, blowing up balloon and after balloon to stretch thin and step inside of, constantly blustering into the only air I can breathe, making blue the rubbery lens that leans me pleura into peritoneum. Pleura and peritoneum are two kinds of serous membranes, fluid-filled sacs that layer around tender organs. If I think of myself as a tender organ, if I think of my blue balloon as a serous membrane, if I think of myself (a liquid) suspended (in liquid), then the emulsion of me has to wonder if I am capable of breathing underwater.

iv.

I continue reading lines from books with blue spines.

Hljómskálagarður Park sits on Tjörnin's southeast corner and has a section dedicated to sculptures by five Icelandic women.[4]

Questions of straightforward power (or survival) ...[5]

v.

I start taking antidepressants when I am fifteen. I go on and off, on and off them for the next twenty-plus years. I don't like taking medication. I am wary of it, critical of it, and, each time after I've stopped taking it, always abruptly, always without my doctor's knowledge, I become entirely forgetful it was ever helpful to me.

This time is different. I've told people: this is helping me. If I tell you I plan to go off this medication, please remind me that I don't really want to. Grab me by the shoulders and give me a shake and say *no, no, no, off this medication, you will not go.* I suspect that even in that self-sabotaging state, I will respond positively to rhyming when, in truth, I know that if I ever decide to stop taking my medication, I will do it without letting anyone know.

When I was fifteen, my doctor prescribed me Paxil. I go back a few days later and tell him I want Prozac because maybe I've watched *Girl, Interrupted,* and read *Prozac Nation,* and Prozac is much sexier than Paxil. I am depressed, and nothing is sexy about that, but I am still an adolescent girl with a penchant for getting the details right.

---

[4] The Blue Lagoon is one of the most visited attractions in Iceland. It is the result of the output from the adjacent Svartsengi geothermal plant and its surreal blue color comes from the fact that it is steeped in silica and sulfur.

[5] But water isn't *really* blue. Water absorbs red, orange, yellow light; when white light from the sun enters ocean or river, mostly blue light is returned. Blue is a love letter sent from water to my eyes.

vi.

This is how a bruise forms:

First, you walk around like your sea legs are strong. The land is something that tips away from you.

Second, you forage under the sink for a vase to put the peonies in; you find one, but you stand up too quickly and hit your head on the bottom of the cupboard. You are perpetually unaware of your surroundings.

Third, is an object in motion approaching another object (in motion).

Fourth, the levees near the delta plain of capillaries break, and there is flooding.

Fifth, isn't it easier to be carried away?

vii.

This is how SSRIs work:

Firstly, it stands for selective serotonin reuptake inhibitor if you've never cared to look it up.

Secondly, stop telling people that smiling releases endorphins that might trick your brain into thinking it's happy. Or is it dopamine? Or something else entirely?

Third, you're going to have to trick yourself.

Fourth, the trick is to trick yourself.

Fifth, the only trick is to try and learn more about the ones that undermine and the ones that help; do less of the first, do more of the second.

viii.

When I am in college, hanging out on the patio of some shitty dive bar with friends and friends of friends, one of them pauses and points at me with his cigarette. *You are a melancholy woman*, he says.

It's startling. To be seen this way in the middle of someone's smoke break. Approaching exactness.

Blood is a blue thing until exposed to oxygen. I cut my nails—hurriedly, haphazardly—to the quick. The body is an uncooked thing being brought to a simmer. When one of my edges is rubbed raw, bruised, or pricked, I bleed blue. *A melancholy woman,* sad at a cellular level.

Sometimes, I have to remind myself that emotions change every 30 seconds. A minute from now, I might be fucking ecstatic. I doubt it.

ix.

The old guy had died a hero; he'd gone down for the Rose Vegetable cause; his actions were the first I'd seen outside a boob tube or movie theater that bore even faint resemblance to Christ's line: "He that loseth his life shall save it."[6]

Yes, but I love to slip the virtue and severity of the noble Romans under the grey light of your eyes, and dancing grasses and summer breezes and the laughter and shouts of boys at play—of naked cabin boys squirting each other with hosepipes on the decks of ships.[7]

x.

This is how blue breaks you open:

Firstly, it is the color of creativity, which, essentially, is the state of constant birth, which tugs words and shapes and heartbeat out of you and into a puddle of water that pools around your feet on the floor.

---

[6] In 1798, George Colman's one-act farce Blue Devils was performed at Theatre Royal in Convent Garden. Blue devils were demon-like spirits thought to impart melancholy and sadness.

[7] In "The Lament of Mars," Mars is heartbroken over Venus "wyth tears blewe and with a wounded herte."

Secondly, it makes you think the puddle of water has nothing to do with you but is seeping up of its own volition from beneath the floor.

Third, it deviates, veins visible beneath deliberately pale skin branch forearm faintly like long afternoon shadows that give nothing away.

Fourth, it is an upstart, headstrong, rare, guttural, and growl—one blue moon after another.

Fifth, it is the splay of forget-me-nots you tap against your prefrontal cortex, trying, trying to remember, closing your blue eyes (same as your mother, same as your grandfather) against the brightness that makes you forget.

xi.

By now, my dosage has increased. I no longer have to bite the second pill in half. I take two full pills. This is nice because the medication tastes incredibly bitter and stains my tongue numb when I have to bite into it. I have increased my dosage, but still find myself in one of my deepest depressions in what feels like forever, though we all know by now that my memory of such things (any things) isn't superb.

When I am in this depression, I work from 8:00 AM to 5:00 PM. I take an Advil PM and sleep from 6:00 PM to 6:30 AM. I don't eat. I skip therapy. I change my phone number as a transubstantiation of disappearance.

I am trying not to cut myself during this depressive state. It is my tried and true way of making my hurt visible, if but to me. I've never been one to make cuts on the parts of my skin that others might see. They are not a dialogue with anyone but myself. Still, I'm ashamed to be a cutter, though not for the reasons you might think. It's such an immature expression… and not only do I—in my late thirties—still cut myself, I came to it well beyond my teens. I should have moved on to some more adult form of self-harm. Something that a proper flagellant would do.

xii.

When I am in college hanging out on the patio of some shitty dive bar with friends, a friend of friends pauses, points at me with his cigarette, and says *you are a melancholy woman*; I feel exposed without warrant, not seen. This same man replied thusly to a female student—some other time, same shitty dive bar—asking to bum a smoke: *how does it feel to want?* After hearing me sing, the same man once told me that I *must make the best sounds during sex.*

xiii.

When I cut myself, I use a pair of scissors open wide. As if they are doing the splits. I press both my hands and the weight of my upper body behind them on top of the scissors. I bend the blade so the sharp edge is angled toward the skin, ideally 45 degrees. I graph x-y coordinates. I scribe longitudinal inclines over my thighs. The result is asymmetrical but balanced from side to side. It's inexact, but so am I.

I am trying not to cut myself during the most recent depressive state for reasons I can't quite ascertain. I don't know. I'm tired. It isn't scratching the itch.

Instead, at odd points during the day, I set a retractable ballpoint pen on my forearm with the point retracted. I click the button at the top of the pen and feel its point push into my skin. I hold it as long as I can. It's a small thing: this act of blue devotion. Its consequence is a small welt encircled by an indentation. It is a poor explanation for what I am feeling, and the sting of the pain goes away entirely too quickly, but I am relieved to experience a hurt I can see. More often than not, I am coded in pain written in milk. I must be held up to the light long enough to decipher the markings but not so long the cipher is forgotten.

xiv.

When I was in college hanging out on the patio of some shitty dive bar with friends, a friend of friends pointed at me with his cigarette and said, *you are a melancholy woman*; I am afraid he is right about me, that I am sad for no reason. Then I remember that he—pontificating lit cigarette one after another—knows nothing but the sound of his voice. I understand this because I know little beyond the sound of my own. I know little beyond the sound of my voice, but I am trying to listen to things that are decidedly not my voice more and more. Each day, or maybe each week… at least every so often, and when I remember that I am submerged, I untie the blue balloon I hold, that holds me. When the knot loosens, an ocean spills out. I let it air dry before filling the balloon with an expectant air, the kind that comes just before lightning, an earthquake, or a tornado, and I breathe into it knowing that something is coming.

13

Eternal Return

I tell my friend that I am feeling existentially opposed to everything today. Fundamentally, he asks? Existentially, I reiterate. As usual, I make it about me. We are at work. We use an oversized calculator to review some numbers because my prior calculations were off by $5,000. It wasn't bad math, but bad typing. I am prone to inexactitude, just as I am guilty of letting autocorrect be another reason my communication skills are lacking.

Later, I searched for a new podcast and, right there, featured and in the forefront, is a show described as "existential exploration." When I point out this kismet to my friend, he says *you should be dancing.*

He might be right, but I am not one for dancing.

My sister and I watch White Christmas every December when we are young. Bing Crosby and Rosemary Clooney are the singers. Danny Kaye and Vera-Ellen Westmeyer Rohe are the dancers. All four of the movie's stars sing and dance in the film, but it's obvious that each pair has a primary talent. To be honest, Vera Ellen doesn't actually sing any of the songs in the film—her parts are either dubbed in by Rosemary Clooney or singer Trudy Stevens. The dancing scenes are not my favorite. I like them well enough, but—as a child—I want talking and singing and jokes and drama. The dancing scenes are not my favorite, but Vera-Ellen is my favorite.

Vera-Ellen is a versatile and powerful dancer. She dances solos with Fred Astaire, Gene Kelly, and Donald O'Connor. She is a Rockette. She performs on Broadway. Vera-Ellen is described as "elfin" and "slim of build." These descriptions are accurate—she is beautiful and charismatic and has a glint of mischief in her eye. She has the tiniest waist I've ever seen. I want to look exactly like her—elfin and lithe. I want to move like she does. I don't know how, though, nor do I think it's possible for me to move like Vera-Ellen or if moving like Vera-Ellen means, to my mind, something more like "looking" like Vera-Ellen. Still, I can't move like her, or like my friend Jess who glides her body up and down on the dance floor, or like the roomful of dancers at the beach in Belize.

The town of Livingston in Belize is named for a large rock just offshore. I'm not sure at what point a rock becomes an island, but this particular one seems shy of the necessary size to gain that distinction. The rock is covered in green things growing, a fecund lighthouse beaming bright and jungled. I remember it. I remember the beach at night. I remember the darkness feeling more profound because of the sound of the ocean waves breaking without me being able to see them break.

I remember all of this because I tell my friend that, one, I am feeling existentially opposed to everything, two, I don't dance and, three, when I do dance, it's in my living room, though, four, my favorite night of dancing was in Livingston.

If you ask me what I believe in, it's this: a person can drown in a tablespoon of water, let alone an entire sea or ocean.

In Livingston, we eat at a restaurant called Maria's that serves Indian food. It is a nice change from el plato tipico: rice, beans, plantains, and cheese. In Guatemala, we eat tipico every day. At Maria's, I eat red curry. Sweat gathers at my hairline as I eat, and I look up to watch the lazy rotation of the ceiling fan. It offers no relief. After dinner, we go dancing. Loud music spills out of a palapa-like structure on the beach with open sides and a palm-thatched roof. Loud music shoots up and out like a natural phenomenon, Old Faithful, a volcano. There is a heartbeat in the music, diastole and systole steady and cycling giving over to, giving life, the burning lung smell of something born into oxygen.

I tell people that I don't dance. Sometimes I tell them that I hate it, but what I hate is the feeling of being in my body, looming and swaying and untucking the hospital corners of bed sheets where some unnamed pains have been tucked in for a rest, a long rest, a fairy tale Sleeping Beauty magical time versus reality time kind of rest. Dancing wakes things up.

My friend goes into an existential rabbit hole. He sends me three different synopses of *The Outsider*. I've never read it, but I point out that living simultaneously as an ascetic while partaking of Dionysian excess (which, according to one of the synopses, is a premise of the book and one of several phases toward absolution of self with something greater) seems conflicted. Then again, I am only skimming the paragraphs. *I need more Dionysian excess,* my friend says. He is the one who wants to go dancing. He asks, *Where do I go dancing?*

I've only been dancing once in this town, entirely against my will. When my friend Jess comes to visit, she has something to prove to someone she left behind, and to prove it, dancing has to happen. I tell her that dancing is literally the last thing I want to do, that it is unpleasant and painful. I tell her I hate it and do not want to go.

We go dancing anyway.

So when my friend asks *Where do I go dancing,* I am not sure what to tell him. The only thing I remember about my night of dancing with Jess is that I survived. And a couple of days later, when we eat bagels, Jess tells me that a jaguar has been visiting her in her dreams. In Mayan mythology, the jaguar may have been the ruler of the underworld. A rough translation of the name (Xibalba) of the underworld is "place of fear," and the jaguar represents ferocity, the ability to face fears. Jess is my jaguar. At least for today.

A belief system is something lipid: liquid suspended in liquid. A human is something like a belief system, all watery and washed through, rowing a boat into a storm.

In the palapa dance hall in Livingston, beautiful bodies gleam vine or mountain, pulsing with the thrust-luck of tiny wing beat movements. The movement is so slight and rapid that the air hums with electricity. As if hip vibrations could generate enough energy to live off the grid.

Jess arrives in town late hell-bent on going dancing. She is trying to prove a point that can only be proven with her body. She is trying to prove a point to someone hundreds of miles away.

We get a late-night snack at the only place I know to serve food at this time. What do I know? Years in, and it's true that I'm still new around here. Jess looks across the table at me with her kind eyes gleaming at their outer edges. Without missing a beat in her story, she says: *Your grandmother is here. Standing right behind you. She's touching your shoulder.*

I tell Jess that not only do I not want to go dancing, dancing is the last thing I want to do. Jess is trying to prove a point that can only be proven with her body, but the point of my daily life has been to slip outside my skin at all times. Trying to slip back inside, trying to claim organs as my own, limbs, the rise, and fall of flesh… trying to knit the substance of me together long enough to move in time to music, to be seen—a wail and a brain and a worry impersonating as a body—is a drowning of sorts. I doubt I'd even try to hold my breath. I'd go deadweight and think only bottom-dwelling thoughts.

Jess sees ghosts. It hasn't always been this way, but something flipped—something inside her, or a someone (a little boy) who came to her—and she has grown comfortable with their regular appearance.

A human can resemble a ghost by paling fade and slipping silently into the background.

One of the songs in White Christmas is called "The Best Things Happen While You're Dancing." *Even those with two left feet come out all right if the girl is sweet,* one of the lyrics goes. Another number pays tribute to vaudeville and pokes at the shift from "dancing" to modern "choreography." Vera-Ellen swirls across the screen, around the stage, making it look easy. I am curious about the rest of her life, but the details I find are too sad to remember.

Later, months later, my friend looked at me in puzzlement. I have just said something about his upcoming vacation. It has given him a sense of déjà vu. We have been here before, he thinks. This conversation. This moment. He mentions Nietzsche's idea of eternal return, and I cry. I am not sure I want to do this again. And again.

A human can resemble a ghost by paling fade and slipping silently into the background. For example, a woman is a slippery thing. A woman is a lipid thing, pooling into a puddle on the ground. She can drown here. She can stay here forever.

14

Notes > After a Forest Fire

Two years after a forest fire > scorched bark peels away from the trees and falls to the ground like a scab shedding off a wound. Gravity compels them. Steam rises out of the twin pipes of the *Prinz Friedrich Wilhelm* and falls back toward the upper deck, toward the 2,519 passengers pitching against one another as something—kin to gravity, perhaps—propels them toward new life. Martin Steenblock boards the ocean liner in Bremen, Germany, under, I imagine, winter skies thick with dark. In the great heaving belly of the ship—bloated hopeful, regretting everything—the moon-pull presses Martin onward, the *Prinz Friedrich Wilhelm* blundering by stars toward new. On March 23, 1909, he passed through Ellis Island. Seventy years and nineteen days later, I was born.

Five years after a forest fire > *epilobium angustifolium* (fireweed) is a pioneer species, pink and persistent, creeping rhizome and confident along the forest floor, leaves spirally arranged and pinnate veined, strong with all the sun, all the water. Like the westward, ho! optimism of destiny—betting on luck and divinity and a desire to live—driven forward into the prairie, vast and silent like the steppes. The people known as the Germans from Russia felt at home there, the grass wind and tickled, the soothing austerity of waking up each day to work.

Six years after a forest fire > the grasses grow in clumps—like wild grass—and send tiny tendrils of root in every direction, slight, but with the power to keep the ground steady. Homesteaders build lives out of the available materials. People like Martin see to the soil.

Sixteen years after a forest fire > seeds freed by smoke and heat spring from the acid duff filling out noble and silver needles ripe like fat babies that arrive year after year. Born with hoes in hand to till and till, to tend the fields surrounding their homes and the towns with names like Ashley and Faith. The children have names like Gottfried and Matildhe, Johann and Lydia, Rueben and Irene, Harry and Bernice, Freidr and Anna.

Twenty-three years after a forest fire > the understory begins to stabilize, and memory of the fire is no longer cognitive in all the green green that crowds for jostle and life, like these families—my family—who scuffed even further west, to the continental edge, transplants or something like them, looking to thrive in the calm of wide streets with a laundry line out back, a fence out front, and happy—their wide-eyed children growing up wont to want. Contentment can be a thing raisined and sucrose. Martin distills his family into something sunny and new.

Forty years after a forest fire > the ground begins to cool. I don't yet exist. Still, the parts of me that exist (with names like grandfather, grandmother, and so on) have histories (theirs, Martin's, Gustav's, Christina's) that they aren't sure how to discuss. Everyone speaks English now. Still, the parts of me that did exist then have this to say to me now: heat lingers when you are born from it; death is a re-imagination of birth; a name carries a particular fate.

Fifty-six years after a forest fire > some, not all, of the charred spines are gnawed nimble and felled by the mouths fury of insect banter, and the forest is defined by slash but also by the puzzle piece bark that, when loosened and sniffed, tugs olfactory vanilla and sweet, like organ music and biscuits Dorothea Steenblock makes Sunday dinner around the maple table, where folly and plumb lucky big-smile children sit with their parents and their grandparents and the song home rushes from a red crystal decanter.

Eighty-two years after a forest fire > heartwood tender rings slowly like a drum (deep) thump accruing boom-like and expansive, the wail of an unruly loud-cry child is born of the big-smile children, and sound equates to birth, a low moan over water rumbles thunder and true. I am born. I am born into so much. I am born feeling the moon-pull of ocean passages.

Ninety years after a forest fire > I am looking for my people… Martin is dead. Most of his children are dead. His grandchildren have forgotten what they knew of the trip on the *Prinz Friedrich Wilhelm* just as Martin had forgotten about the journeys of his great-greats. Still, I think this has to do with the *Prinz Friedrich Wilhelm* being renamed four times. Or that, by now, its seaworthy days have ended, scrapped in Italy under an alias.

Ninety-nine years after a forest fire > the trees are growing, grown, and once again, speaking underground their subterranean language of fungi and love and fear, musky parables of how to live after a burn. With the light filtering through the canopy, I can see a scar on my arm, one I didn't know I had. I move my arm back and forth, and the scar—pale and burnished—glitters as it catches the light.

One hundred and nineteen years after a forest fire > I walk through a charred forest collecting charcoal rubbings from tree trunks. I study them later at home, knowing they are x-rays of what happened there. What happened to me?

One hundred and twenty years after a forest fire > I wake with the sunrise. I am diurnal and somewhat flammable—formed by hope, prairie, desperation, divinity, steppes, ocean, moon-pull, heaving, the scar, leaving, and leaving—a prophyte practicing rising from the ashes daily. Everywhere I go, my feet are covered in soot.

15

A Girl Forgotten

Some autobiographical works can only be accessed through fiction. This is why she calls herself by many names. She wants to see what sounds right.

A girl who is forgotten learns to forget herself. This is why there are so many notebooks. She writes herself each day only to be erased at night. She calls herself names to see which one sounds right. *Mab* sticks sometimes. Queen of dreams. Knowing the difference between sleeping and waking can be hard for her.

Not long ago, she dreamt that she had been dreaming. In her dream, a friend asks her something. *I dreamt that* she says; I *knew you would say that.* But even the dream itself is a dream.

Knowing the difference between sleeping and waking can be hard for her. This is why she sends her dream synopses to a friend most mornings. She wants a second opinion.

When she is young, she is left behind in a garden in the summertime. She has never been in a cornfield, but the metaphor applies. The scale of the towering sunflowers and hollyhocks to her tiny toddler body tells her she is lost forever. When she is remembered, they find her by the sweet peas tangled in sweetness, pale pink, and burgundy. She has plied her senses to forget. Forgetfulness begets forgetting.

Here is a story about her:

She was born of a hillside, grass pungent with morning dew. There is a good wolf standing watch. They are each watchful: silent, quiet, still, waiting.

Or:

She was born north of where she grew up. It's true that she could walk immediately, and immediately she walked away, out into the parking lot in front of the birthing center. She wondered why trees were alone and sequestered behind cement curbs in the sea of cars.

Or:

She is born saying *I wish I could breathe underwater.* She is born saying *this is a fish,* or *I am riverine and finned—cutthroat, golden, redband.* Standing at the edge of a river, taken in by the sound of water interrupted by rock, she could find that she is lipid and sustained, foaming riparian and growing her own gills. A person easily suggestible and highly contaminated by the swoon of her surroundings might even slip Parr-Smolt and silver from freshwater to saltwater and back again.

She tells herself tiny fictions. She gives herself many names and comes up with various origin stories. Sometimes, these are all she has.

16

Pandora in July

I have always felt a kinship with Pandora. Was it curiosity that prompted her to open the jar that Epimetheus left out in the open? Did he leave it out in the open, or did she go looking? Either way, I won't point a finger at her. I won't lay the blame where the story asks me to lay it. Of course, she was beautiful, whatever that meant. She was born of a time that didn't bother discussing women who weren't beautiful. That time is also now.

And, yes, it was a jar, not a box. A jar filled with evil, or so the story goes. And what is evil, exactly? The evil—as it was contained in the jar—was not specified. Aside from "sickness" and "death," it's hard to say what else was there. Trans fats? Chain letters? The words "I promise?"

Though they share a name, the pandora moth—Coloradia pandora—is different: a forest insect the size of a toddler's hand, dappled and furred, with smudges of a pale rouge on the hindwings. Adults have a large body bedecked with layer after layer of tiny fringe. Their forewings are darker, more extensively patterned than their hindwings. The latter is lighteris w—whiteish, grey, and with the aforementioned pink. Pandora Pinemoth—part of me imagines this to be the perfect nom de plume for the writer of a very specific kind of book.

In the summer of 2017, Pandora Moths returned to Central Oregon, where I still live. I had just spent my first winter in Bend, and it had been long, harsh, and excessive. The late spring melt had forced robins to source most of their food above ground. All over town, they were gathering—mawkish and maudlin—getting drunk off of the fermented berries from the mountain ash tree. Now the moths. They're back; people said each time they saw a moth fluttering in front of their faces. It was all gently apocalyptic. As if the world were coming to an end, but entirely without urgency.

Pandora moths are distinctive because of their size and because they arrive en masse and hang out in large groups like the robins in the mountain ash trees. This is called swarming, flocking, or herding, and it is a form of self-organization, a collective behavior seen in animals that aggregate together. For insects, the right word is swarming. A swarm is swarming—the phrase alone carries a feeling of foreboding.

The similarities between Pandora and Eve are obvious, both harbingers of evil. Consider this: when I was a child, I spoke as a child, I understood as a child, I thought as a child. And what occurred to me then was that the idea of heaven was terrifying. Perhaps it's my mercurial nature, but I've never been one for constant pleasantness, 80-degree weather year-round, or even streets shiny with gold. It sounded like a place where everyone was on Quaaludes, and while I didn't hope for the alternative, I was convinced heaven wasn't a good option. Seduced by sameness—that's never been my way.

I wonder, when Pandora opened the lid to the jar, did a swarm of something fly out? What do unspecified things and sickness and death and evil look like? Were they so numerous that they blotted out the sun, even for a moment, causing everyone within a mile of Pandora to shriek, wail, moan, and pull out their hair in tufted clumps and stomp their feet against the cracked earth?

It's becoming clear to me now that who I am on the page is a harbinger of who I am off the page. Here's what I start to notice—I can talk about things I've written about first. For example, I can say the words *I'm sorry or don't know,* or *This is why I want to hold you until you burst under the Tungsten glow of my love.* Because how can you start to live off the page and not notice just how much there is to crack your heart open every moment of every day?

I listen to Rachel Zucker's Commonplace podcast episode featuring poet TC Tolbert. *We try things on the page that turn into ways of being in the world…* How am I using the page to practice being in the world? What does the shape of my syntax, the size of my margins and the use of white space (or lack thereof) mean? And—glory to the pantheon of gods—why so many em dashes?

Swarming behavior realizes independent entities working as a collective. A small thing—like a pandora moth—becomes many small things which, in turn, become very large. This very large thing will often show up near outdoor lights. This very large thing will cover the exterior wall of a building or the expanse of a parking lot. When you drive over one, and you can't help but drive over one, you can feel it. As with many things, when you see this very large thing—electric and flickering like a light source itself—you don't know what you're looking at. The eyes have to adjust not only to darkness but to scale. Perspective is everything.

I zoom in and pan out quickly on the page at sharp turns. These transitions—or lack thereof—render an image of my mind as a pinboard for a murder case, a string extended from one picture to another. It makes sense to me—these associations—in a way that linearity and chronology never do. And so, if you look at my words on the page, you will see the following: text blocks like lily pads. They require a leap of faith, yes, but also of the imagination.

Can we get more specific about evil? About the nature of things that could have been let loose from Pandora's jar? Curiosity killed the cat, or so the saying goes. There is a second part to this phrase… did you know? *Curiosity killed the cat, but satisfaction brought it back.* As if to say that curiosity has repercussions, but knowing offers resurrection. The name Pandora means "all-gifted." When the gods created her—the first human woman—Hephaestus molded her out of clay, and the legion of remaining gods bestowed gifts upon her. She was punishment, you see. She was the revenge exacted on humanity for the theft of fire by Epimetheus' brother Prometheus. The gods all chipped in to bestow her with gifts, namely "seductive gifts." Do you see now? Pandora was set up.

It is thought that the etymology of the word evil stems from upelo-, a derivative of the Indo-European upo- or upa-, and originally meant something that "exceeded its limits." If this is true, then the evils in the jar that came to be in Pandora's possession were already bursting at the seams.

Let's review the facts. Pandora was fashioned out of clay and given as a gift—the first human woman—to Epimetheus. Soon after, immediately after, she opened a jar that unleashed evil upon humanity. Though she may have been curious to see what was inside the jar, the contents were a punishment for all of humanity, punishment premeditated by Zeus after Prometheus stole fire. Of course, the messenger (in this case, Pandora) was—in a predictable sleight of hand—responsible for the contents. As if to say… if only she hadn't been so fucking beautiful. If only Hephaestus hadn't begun with the smoothest, petal-soft ratio of clay to water; if only he hadn't sung low like a valley when he formed her hips, licked pale and wanting at the mountains when he fashioned her breasts. In the end, fault is always found with the seductress.

The pandora moth has a two-year life cycle. Is this something that you want to know? The pandora moth lives focused and frenzied for two years. All the pandora moth knows of the world are ponderosa pines and the volcanic-formed soil beneath them.

Adult moths mate during the summer. The eggs incubate for around 40 days and then hatch into larvae that feed on foliage before overwintering at the base of the needles. Come spring, the larvae continue their feast through late June, with an appetite so ravenous that, depending upon their population size, areas of the forest are defoliated.

Death and birth, death and rebirth. The contents of the jar cannot be put back in the jar, and thus the life cycle of humanity emerges. Or so the story goes. Though earlier versions of the story could have been different, very different. The jar may have contained only good things.

This makes me wonder when, exactly, Pandora was brought to life. I can relate to her, you know. Not to mix myths, but I have been considering the fact that I might be my own Pygmalion, sculpting myself out of clay and eventually falling in love with the form uncovered. He sculpted a woman to love. Am I not doing the same?

For the sake of dramatic effect, evil should be introduced during a time akin to perfection, at least perfection as many of you see it: 80-degree weather and the like. In other words, summer. In other words, July. Can you imagine it? A beautiful woman kneels on the ground in front of a jar. It is lidded and—as when her lids are heavy and shut—she lifts it and opens to the world with a boom-singe like thunder, like lightning. Apocalyptic, those around her may have thought, the sky ripped open and the swarm of pestilence, evils vague and defined, death, even, blotted out the sun. This is the kind of thing that could only happen in July.

It's true. In a way, I am conjuring myself. It's true that I am molding myself out of clay. In aggregate, I am a conglomeration of gifts from the gods fumbling foolishly through my life.

In philosophy and systems theory, emergence refers to a state when a whole is greater than the sum of its parts. This is why swarming pandora moths are a sight to see — beguiling, perhaps a little frightening. In emergence, the whole has traits that the independent entities do not have. Perhaps this shows up in how the collective moves or behaves. All I can say is that it's weird to suddenly become the small thing, to have scale shift so rapidly as to transfix the human tiny, staring at the moths en masse.

The very large thing that is a swarm has the power to make you feel inconsequential. Like a rapid zoom or pan, an immediate perspective change is dizzying, disorienting. As if to say: you, you there! You are not as in control as you might think. The trick of these perspective shifts is Dramamine and attention. It is good to be curious about what you notice. Is it Michelangelo who talks about art as uncovering what was always there? Maybe every artist, especially every sculptor, says this. And probably they are right.

When Pandora and I hang out, we laugh a lot. We crack each other up. Sometimes, after the bottle of wine is gone and the light of day is fading, I'll slip in a serious question. *Do I feel like I've been misunderstood?* She repeats. Usually, she stares off into the distance, not, like you might think, toward the sunset. Instead, Pandora looks toward the East because she *likes to remember where things came from, not where they end up.* She says the opposite at sunrise—she *wants to see where things will end.* Since she never answers my question with anything but a shrug and a wink and a stretch as she stands to go and grab more wine, I take this to mean that she, one, isn't sure anyone can ever really understand anyone else, and, two, if you want to try you have to look in the opposite direction.

After the feast, the pandora moths' larvae emerge from the trees and burrow into the soil. The adult moth emerges the following summer, and the cycle continues. Where I live, adult moths are seen in odd-numbered years, larvae, and defoliation in even-numbered years. During outbreaks, even larger numbers of the pandora moth can be found. Outbreaks last for 3 or 4 generations. Next summer, the adult moths will rise once again from the dirt, not unlike Pandora herself. Is this why they share a name? I can't find any literature that confirms this theory, and she has no idea, but the poetry of it appeals to me.

This is another way I come to be on the page—one thing resembling another and me, working so hard to pull taut a string between them, me zooming in, then out, me walking around the words like they are sculptures I must see from every angle, me reaching out my hand to touch them even though a tiny sign politely requests that I refrain. I have to know things this way, which is to say the only way I can approach anything is by not knowing.

All that time, all the hiding myself from myself on the page... if it's hide-and-seek I've been playing, then I am either getting worse at hiding or better at seeking. *Maybe both?* Pandora chimes in. *Maybe both,* I agree.

What about the pathos mistranslation? I try again. Pandora never takes the bait. A *pithos* is a large storage vessel, aka a jar. *If they changed a jar into a box, what else did they get wrong?* I ask. *Or did they get anything right?* It's true that Pandora is beautiful, though not in the ways you might think. She is earthen and radiant. She pupates in the ground each night and leaves smudges of dirt with each step she takes. She leaves a trail of iron-rich clay when she flicks away a mosquito from my arm. The orange stripe makes me feel like a warrior. *We can fight this*, I say, but Pandora looks through me, taken in by the reflective glow of the sunset behind her.

Swarming comes from chaos. It is spontaneous—the actions of these individual entities that suddenly seek to comprise a whole. It is spontaneous and beautiful and precise and unplanned. It can only come from chaos. It can only emerge from something inchoate—a lump of clay—to transform into something akin to perfection. Something like Pandora.

And I couldn't look at it directly, the blank page. I couldn't look at it. I had to look at those marks of ink askance, arms akimbo, holding myself together, sending forth filament and thread. Then, a flash. A glimpse of something finned and silver moving in and out of serif trunks: *me*? I wondered. Am I no longer the girl who erases herself each night? Am I, instead, revealed by my writing, and that's where the story ends?

V. Joshua Adams, Scott Shibuya Brown, Brian Rivka Clifton, Brittney Corrigan, Jessica Cuello, Barbara Cully, Alison Cundiff, Neil de la Flor, Suzanne Frischkorn, Victoria Garza, Reginald Gibbons, Joachim Glage, Caroline Goodwin, Kathryn Kruse, Meagan Lehr, Brigitte Lewis, Jenny Magnus, D.K. McCutchen, Jean McGarry, Rita Mookerjee, Mamie Morgan, Alexis Orgera, Karen Rigby, Jo Salas, Maureen Seaton, Kristine Snodgrass, Cornelia Maude Spelman, Peter Stenson, Melissa Studdard, Curious Theatre, Gemini Wahhaj, Megan Weiler, Cassandra Whitaker, David Wesley Williams

jacklegpress.org

www.ingramcontent.com/pod-product-compliance
Lightning Source LLC
Chambersburg PA
CBHW031250120626
46545CB00007B/2740